SO-DFI-084

Summit

Marc Maurer
Editor

Large Type Edition

A KERNEL BOOK
published by
NATIONAL FEDERATION OF THE BLIND

TABLE OF CONTENTS

EDITOR'S INTRODUCTION

Summit is a word that is rich with multiple meanings. It can mean the highest point of a mountain, the highest degree of achievement, or a meeting of officials at the highest level.

Blindness also is a word that summons to the imagination many thoughts, though usually not the lofty and exalted notions associated with the word *summit*. Why, then, you may wonder, did we choose to name this twenty-second volume in the Kernel Book Series *Summit*?

We did so for a very simple reason: No other name would be appropriate for this particular book. This is so because in May 2001, Erik Weihenmayer, one of our members who is totally blind, led a team of

Marc Maurer, President
National Federation of the Blind

mountain climbers to the summit of Mt. Everest. And later, I, as President of the organization which believed in Erik enough to make his Everest Expedition a reality, was invited along with Erik to meet with the highest official of our country, President George W. Bush.

This second summit—our meeting with the President of the United States—did more than merely congratulate Erik on his magnificent achievement. It recognized the work and spirit of the National Federation of the Blind.

When we decided to join with Erik in helping him to achieve his dream of climbing to the summit of Mt. Everest, we were often asked why we would commit the organization to such a seemingly bizarre effort.

If he had failed (and especially if he had been seriously injured), both our organization and the work we are trying to accomplish would have been enormously damaged—set back perhaps for decades. There is no better way to answer that question than to look to Erik's own eloquent words. I suspect that those of you who read them here will find them as inspiring and compelling as did those of us in the National Federation of the Blind when we decided to back the Everest Expedition.

For Erik to reach the summit of Mt. Everest required unflagging courage, tremendous physical strength and sacrifice, and an undauntable mental attitude. He did not go alone. He was accompanied in spirit by many, many thousands more— blind people from every corner of the United States, who had dreamed with him, hoped with him, prayed for him.

We believed in him, in his capacity to understand the danger, to plan (along with others) the expedition, to carry his load and do his part in dealing with the challenges of the climb itself, and to bring the plan to its ultimate success. His faith is our faith; his spirit is our spirit; his extraordinary exploit exemplifies the organized blind movement. Not many blind people (or for that matter sighted people) will ever climb Everest, but all of us have our own mountains to conquer—perhaps not as dramatic, perhaps not as spell-binding, perhaps not as captivating to the world-at-large; but in the lives of those who climb them, just as compelling as Mt. Everest.

Here are just some of the other blind "mountain climbers" you will meet in this latest volume of the Kernel Book series: a blind college student worrying about meeting the challenges of his summer job as a camp counselor, a blind grandmother who wants to share storybooks with her baby granddaughter, a teen-ager fearing the loss of physical freedom she thought would necessarily accompany the loss of eyesight, and a second-grader hurt by his school teacher's obvious disdain for her blind students.

We in the National Federation of the Blind look to Erik as the objective symbol of a pioneering organization dedicated to ensuring that blind people everywhere have the opportunity to go where no other blind people have been before.

And we look to you, the friends we have made through the Kernel Books, to help us continue to climb our own mountains. We believe that with your help all of us can reach the summit.

Marc Maurer
Baltimore, Maryland
2002

WHY LARGE TYPE?

The type size used in this book is 14 point for two important reasons: One, because typesetting of 14-point or larger complies with federal standards for the printing of materials for visually impaired readers, and we want to show you what type size is helpful for people with limited sight.

The second reason is that many of our friends and supporters have asked us to print our paperback books in 14-point type so they too can easily read them. Many people with limited sight do not use Braille. We hope that by printing this book in a larger type than customary, many more people will be able to benefit from it.

SUMMIT

by Marc Maurer

I have been fascinated with the thought of the White House for most of my life. I do not know how sighted people react to this building and the symbolism it represents, but I, a blind person, have been attracted to it and to the Oval Office, which is the center of it. Although it has been my good fortune to visit the White House several times, I had not been invited into the Oval Office until July of 2001.

In the spring of 2001, the National Federation of the Blind sponsored an attempt by a blind mountain climber, Erik Weihenmayer, to scale Mount Everest. On May 25, 2001, the attempt reached its climax. Erik Weihenmayer became the first, and so far the only, blind person to stand on the top of the world.

He put together a team of seasoned mountain climbers. He planned the expedition, and he gathered the talent and resources to finish the ascent. He was encouraged and supported by the National Federation of the Blind. Blind men, women, and children across America followed his progress with fascination as he proceeded up the dangerous peak.

When he completed the difficult feat and returned home to the United States, he was welcomed by thousands of well-wishers, and thousands more listened to his description of the exploit at the Convention of the National Federation of the Blind. Most blind people do not climb mountains, but some do. However, all blind people have challenges that come to them, and we all must possess at least some element of the spirit that makes it possible for the blind to climb the mountains.

Erik Weihenmayer and Dr. Marc Maurer

On July 26, 2001, Erik Weihenmayer, a number of other Everest climbers on the National Federation of the Blind's Everest expedition, my wife Patricia, and I were invited to visit the President of the United States in the Oval Office. It was a hot day with a forecast for rain. We had been instructed to wait outside the grounds on the sidewalk immediately next to the gate.

Apparently, identification cards needed to be checked before each of us would be admitted to the grounds. I hoped it would not rain because I was wearing my customary business uniform—a wool suit with a starched white shirt. It is hard to look presentable after standing in the rain. I suspect that these are some of the worries that many people have when waiting for an important event.

I also wondered what would happen in the White House. Would the President be called away to other business? Would he be hurried and abstracted? Would he be polite without being really interested in what we had to say? What would he want us to know? How much time could we expect? What would the arrangements be like? What did I want the President to learn? How could I best present the information? Would I have time for one question, one comment, or more than one? These and dozens of other questions ran through my mind as we waited.

At about 2:40, we were ushered through the gate into the White House grounds. Our credentials had been checked by the guards. After a short walk we came to the building itself, and we went inside. Each of us passed through a metal detector, and we were shown through a reception area into a large room (probably twenty feet wide by thirty-five feet long) containing a sizeable conference table and many chairs. We were informed that the room had been used by President Franklin Roosevelt for many of his important diplomatic gatherings.

At 3:00, we were invited into the Oval Office, which was just down the hall from the conference room where we had been waiting. When I visit a new place, I am always interested in what I can feel. By this I mean not only the atmosphere of my surroundings—the acoustical experience of being in a room—but also the impression I get from the artifacts that I can touch.

For example, the door to the Oval Office is thicker than the doors in modern office buildings. The latch and the locking mechanism on the door are mounted on the surface of the wood. This kind of construction was typical for America during the time of the Revolutionary War. Today, latches and locking mechanisms for doors are placed within the door itself. This suggests that the door to the Oval Office and the hardware on the door are quite old.

I wondered as I touched them how security for the Oval Office is maintained. Modern office buildings have sophisicated locking devices. Of course, it may be that locks are unimportant for the Oval Office because of the surveilance systems in the White House. But I wondered.

I had only fleeting moments to touch these things because we did not have time to stop. Nevertheless, this door enhanced the feeling of tradition that I felt when entering the office of our Chief Executive.

The President was not in the office when we arrived, but he entered almost immediately. He introduced himself to each of us, and urged us to examine his desk and the other furnishings in the office. He said that each President has the opportunity to select the furnishings for the office. The desk of the President had been a gift from Queen Victoria. A British ship had been trapped in a mass of ice in the North Atlantic. An American naval vessel rescued the crew and saved the British ship. Queen Victoria demonstrated the gratitude of Britain by having a desk made from some of the planking from the British ship. She presented the desk to the President of the United States.

The President's desk has also been used by President Theodore Roosevelt and President John F. Kennedy. President Franklin Roosevelt, who used the desk, added a panel to the front of it to prevent others from observing his cripled legs. The panel on the front of the desk is carved with the Presidential Seal.

President Bush quickly moved from a discussion of the furnishings of the Oval Office to other matters. He told us that he was proud and pleased to represent the United States in international negotiations because he knew the spirit of Americans. He felt that this spirit and the deep commitment of Americans to be decent to each other and our neighbors, along with a determination to build a better, more harmonious world, makes America a worthy partner in world affairs. Because of what Americans are, the

President felt honored to be our representative.

He also told us that serving as President is not a simple thing for the members of his family. His children cannot understand the pressures that are placed either on the President or on the members of his family. They know that the job is important, but they do not appreciate the demands it necessarily places on them.

The President was not complaining, he was just talking with us about his family and the nature of the job. It was clear from the conversation that he loved his family and had sympathy for the pressures brought to bear in their lives but that he also knew that the Presidency was so important that it must be served, even if it did bring pressure on those he loved.

To do the job the way he wants it done, President Bush felt that he himself must have a substantial measure of discipline. He expects others who work with him to share this discipline. One element of this discipline is physical fitness. The President knows that we need him to be healthy—he exercises every day.

The President also told us about interaction with members of Congress. He said that the Oval Office is a magical place. People sometimes think that they will go to the White House to give the President a piece of their minds. When they enter the Oval Office, their demeanor changes. Instead of telling the President what they think of him, they say "Mr. President, how are you feeling today?"

We talked with the President about the aspirations of blind people to engage in all kinds of activities, including climbing the most challenging mountains. I discussed our need for the blind to have more education and more instruction in the use of Braille. I talked about a program to increase availability of Braille through distribution of Braille labels to all blind people that can be affixed to ordinary household products. I said that the spirit of independence that has made America a great nation is shared by blind Americans and that we want to participate in building our country as much as anybody else.

The President told us that he admired our determination and supported our efforts. Then, he indicated that we were invited to have pictures taken with him. The White House photographer took these pictures.

After thirty minutes of meeting the leader of the free world, we were escorted back to the reception area. A General from the Joint Chiefs of Staff was waiting. The business of the President must continue. However, President Bush was genuine, realistic, and caring, with a personality to understand the problems faced by each individual, while at the same time being able to handle matters of global scope. I felt completely at ease with our President. I felt completely certain that he would bear the mantle of our Presidency with distinction.

I left the Oval Office feeling more confidence in America and the American system than I had felt when I entered it. At least in part I felt this confidence because our President truly wants blind people and the National Federation of the Blind to be successful. He wants this for us in the same way that he wants it for everybody who possesses the determination to seek independence.

I feel certain that I will not agree with the President all of the time. However, I feel equally certain that I will respect the President's opinions and actions. Our President is worthy of respect.

The President of the United States cannot think about blind people all of the time, and he should not—although he should think about us some of the time, as indeed he does. Fortunately we have the National

Federation of the Blind to concentrate on the problems that blind people face. We can give to them our full attention.

Sometimes we try to help blind children get books. Sometimes we support blind adults looking for work. Sometimes we give training in the way that the blind use specialized tools such as the white cane or Braille. Sometimes we assist with high adventure. We even help some of our friends and colleagues learn that they can conquer the most intractable mountains in the world. Be it a big or little thing if it helps the blind to find hope, we intend to be a part of it. Not all of us will climb mountains, but every one of us has our own peaks to conquer. With your help we can attain the summit.

TO CLIMB EVERY MOUNTAIN

by Erik Weihenmayer

Erik Weihenmayer is a member of the National Federation of the Blind. As he prepared to climb Mt. Everest he spoke to his blind brothers and sisters in the organization, trying to express what the climb meant to him and what it could mean for all of us. As he put it, climbing solo isn't the best way to climb a mountain, and it isn't the best way to improve the lives of blind people, either. Here is what he had to say:

In 1996 my friends and I climbed a rock face, actually the tallest exposed granite monolith in the world, called El Capitan. It's 3,300 feet of overhanging rock in Yosemite Valley in California. The scariest part of the climb was actually sleeping on the ledges. They were maybe a foot-and-a-half wide, and even though you'd lash

Photo by Didrik Johnck © 2001

On the summit - Mt. Everest

yourself to the side of the rock face, you'd still roll over in the night, and, with half your body hanging off a thousand-foot cliff, you wouldn't sleep very well.

In 1995 we climbed Mount McKinley, which is a twenty-thousand-foot peak, the tallest peak in North America. It's also one of the coldest mountains in the world. If you spit near the top of Mount McKinley, your spit will be frozen by the time it hits the ground. It took us twenty-one days with no showers, but we summited on Helen Keller's birthday, which was really special.

Just last January my friend Rick Morris and I summited a peak called Aconcagua (23,000 feet) and the tallest peak in South America. We had this great system that I devised; I thought I was so smart. I connected these bells to Chris's pack and to his ice ax so that, as he climbed in front of me, I could follow him. But, when we left at four in the morning and got up to about 21,000 feet, this horrendous wind screaming off the

Pacific Ocean was blowing straight in our faces—my finger tips were cold; my feet were cold. I couldn't hear the bells anymore, and I thought I was going to have to turn back. But Chris every five minutes or so, knowing I couldn't hear the bells, he'd put his fingers in his mouth and whistle at the top of his lungs. So for three or four hours we played this bizarre game of Marco Polo on the mountain.

When I got to the top of the mountain, it was amazing; I touched this metal cross that somebody had dragged up there and planted on the top. Though blindness might have slowed me down in certain situations on the mountain, I try not to see it as disappointing or sad or tragic. I see my blindness as something that makes my life an adventure. I know that you folks do the same.

I embraced this spirit of adventure when I was in high school. I went out looking for a summer job, and I decided that I could be a dish washer. I went out to a restaurant and asked for a job, and the person said, "Erik, we'd love to hire you, but our kitchen is way too small. You'd bump into things; you'd break things; you wouldn't know how to put things away. We'd love to hire you, but it would be dangerous, so we can't." I went to a bigger restaurant with a really big kitchen this time, and I asked them for a job. They said, "We'd love to hire you, Erik, but our kitchen is way too big. You wouldn't know where to put things away. You'd lose your way in the kitchen, and it might be dangerous."

So I thought, now I can't go wrong. I went to a medium-sized restaurant with a medium-sized kitchen, and I asked for a job, and they said, "Erik, we'd love to hire you, but our pots are way too hot; our dishes come in too fast. You wouldn't be able to keep up." And I never got a job that summer, but I did learn something very valuable which has helped me in my life: people's perceptions of blindness are often more limiting than blindness itself.

You see, before that I thought that, with my own actions, with my own individual efforts, and with the strength of my own will, I could shape people's perceptions about me. I learned that sometimes it takes more than just one person's individual efforts. Sometimes it takes all of us working together, with an organization like the National Federation of the Blind providing a foundation and the necessary leadership to enable all of us simultaneously bashing our heads against these barriers to find the force to break through and feel the sun on our faces.

I think sometimes those external barriers transform into internal barriers, which are the most powerful of all. I learned about these on a training climb for Mount McKinley. We got up to a glacier called the Mere Glacier. It was getting really cold. A storm was coming in, and I was assigned to set up the tents. I had a major problem because I had never set up this kind of tent before. I had always set them up with someone else. I found that, when I laid this tent out in front of me and tried to orient the sleeves and loops and corners of the tent with thick mountaineering gloves on, I was blind in two ways. I couldn't do it.

Finally my friends had to come bail me out and set the tent up for me. I was frustrated and embarrassed. Later I went back to Phoenix, where I lived at the time, I took the tent to a field near my house, and I worked with my thick mountaineering gloves on, breaking it down and setting it up and breaking it down again. I could hear cars slowing down looking at this idiot out in the field in 105-degree weather in a tank top and mountaineering gloves, setting up a winter mountaineering tent. But by the time I got to Mt. McKinley, I could set up tents in any conditions.

Sometimes there is a very blurry line between the things we cannot do and the

Photo by Didrik Johnck © 2001

Crossing a crevasse.

things we can do. I've had a lot of fun over these last years as a blind adventurer, sort of blurring that line even further.

Before I became blind, I remember seeing this picture of a person climbing a frozen waterfall. He was a tiny speck against a massive white wall.

When I became blind, I decided that a blind person could learn how to do this, but I was told by an expert that you can't indiscriminately swing your sharp ice tools (which attach you to the wall) at the ice face. You'd knock giant chunks of ice off which would come down and hurt you.

But I found through trial and error that I could tap my ice tools very lightly against the face and by listening for a certain sound, a certain pitch, I would know whether it was going to be a safe hit or whether it would be a hit that would shatter ice on top of me. See, people thought you had to be able to see to ice climb; they didn't know that there were other ways of doing it.

Just recently we climbed a thousand-meter wall of ice called Polar Circus in the Canadian Rockies, and halfway through the climb I took my glove off and ran my hand across the surface of the ice. It was as cold and smooth as a window on a winter's day. I had to take a deep breath because of the beauty I was feeling at the tips of my fingers. Many sighted people believe that the human eye is the only pathway to beauty, but we know that's just not true.

Before I climbed El Capitan—I didn't want to climb it as a token blind person, where you're dragged to the top of the mountain and spiked on top like a football—I wanted to climb it an honest way. I didn't want to be a token.

I had always followed a rope so, if I had fallen, I would have just dangled. Now I went out and learned how to lead. It's called taking the sharp end of the rope. What enables a team to get up a rock face is that each person takes it in turn to lead the team up the crack system. Your hands and feet are jammed into cracks, and you take various sized pieces of metal gear off your harness and jam them into the crack. As you go a little higher, you take your rope, which is hanging below your harness, and clip it into those pieces of gear. If you fall, you hope those pieces of gear will lock against the crack so you won't fall very far. I learned to lead. I led about a thousand feet, about a third of El Capitan.

All of us do the things we do because we love to do them, because of our passion for that activity. But I would be lying if I didn't admit that a tiny bit of the fun for me is shaping perceptions about what's possible and what's not.

Each of you knows that the best way to shape people's perceptions about blindness is to take the sharp end of the rope, to

Straight up the ice face.

embrace that pioneering spirit of adventure, and demonstrate the capabilities of blind people through our actions. You know what I'm talking about, whether you're the first blind lawyer to set up a private practice in your community or the first blind teacher to be hired in your school district or the first blind person in your college to take a high-level finance class. In many ways each of us is a pioneer embarking into uncharted territory.

Who understands this philosophy, this pioneering spirit, better than the National Federation of the Blind? Throughout its history it has been providing the foundation and leadership for all of us to fulfill our dreams. That is why the NFB has chosen to sponsor this 2001 climb of Mt. Everest once and for all to prove without a doubt that, given the right opportunity and skill and mindset, and backed by the most powerful blindness organization in the world, a blind person can climb to the top of the world.

I believe that, if a blind person is seen succeeding safely on an arduous peak like this one, it won't just shape people's perceptions of blindness; it will shatter them. The exciting part is that, when those perceptions are rebuilt, many, many blind people will find themselves living their lives with greater opportunity.

Part of the fun of climbing for me is that you're roped together. When you're traveling up a glacier, you have these little holes in the snow called crevasses. They can be hundreds of feet deep. They can be thirty feet across. Many times there is just a little frozen snow bridge linking one side to the other. So roped together, one by one, the team crosses over the bridge. As each person crosses, the other teammates get ready to throw their ice axes into the snow to arrest the person if he or she pops through the snow bridge.

It's pretty exciting, but it's scary at the same time. Climbing solo is a really good

Photo by Didrik Johnck © 2001

Eric Weihenmayer

way to wind up being frozen in the bottom of a crevasse. We know that climbing solo on a mountain isn't the best way to cross a glacier. We know as well that climbing solo is not the best way to improve the lives of blind people.

On this NFB rope team, even though we move in sync, each of us is fulfilling unique and vital functions on the team. If you can envision fifty thousand, a hundred thousand blind people all moving together on one mission, toward one dream, but each fulfilling a unique and vital function on the team, then you can envision the scope and the power of the NFB. It will take each of us working together, helping each other, each person doing what he or she can, that will enable us to climb this mountain into first-class citizenship.

We will shape and shatter and rebuild what it means to be blind in this world. I want to end by saying that I'm very proud and very honored to be joining this illustrious rope team with such pioneering legends as Dr. tenBroek, Dr. Jernigan, and Dr. Maurer, I am proud to be working with each of you as we prepare for the historic climb in 2001. Wish us good fortune.

JORDYN'S BOOKSHELF

By Ramona Walhof

Ramona Walhof serves as Secretary of the National Federation of the Blind. Long-time Kernel Book readers will remember her many previous stories, including one about raising her own children as a young widow, which appeared in our very first Kernel Book, What Color is the Sun. *She has recently become a proud grandmother. Here she writes about her new granddaughter, Jordyn:*

I had been out of town on business when my granddaughter was born, and I was most anxious to see her. So I planned to spend Labor Day at my son's house to begin to get acquainted with the baby and the new routine. Jordyn Kathryn was just one week old. The birth had gone well, and the new Mom and Dad seemed to be in control. I brought my knitting and told them not to

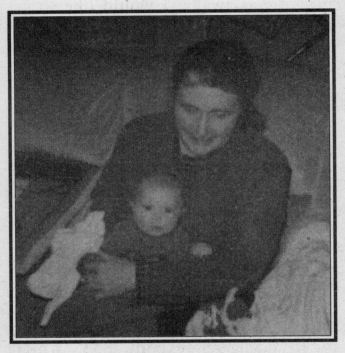

Ramona Walhof and Jordyn

worry about entertaining me, but when Jordyn was awake, I would like to get acquainted. Jordyn weighed 7 pounds one ounce at birth and was as tiny as you would expect and very active. She twisted and stretched and grunted and snuggled just the way she should.

She also had lots of company. While I was there, friends came in with a three-month-old baby. This child seemed huge compared to Jordyn, and I was glad to have her on my lap for a while. I had brought a book about the big red dog, Clifford, which had a series of buttons on the side causing all sorts of sounds and voices.

While I held the older baby, I picked up the book for a little entertainment. I could not read it. All I could do was turn the pages and push the buttons and talk to the baby, but she was fascinated. Several people commented on how interested she was. She did not need to understand the story to enjoy the sounds and bright pictures. But it would have been more fun for me actually to read the book.

As Jordyn grew older, I knew I would want some books I could really read.

When my own children were small (thirty years ago) we borrowed books from the library built by Dr. Kenneth Jernigan when he directed programs for the blind in Iowa. There were many books for small children with both print and Braille text side by side along with pictures. These books had been produced by the American Action Fund for Blind Children and Adults. The Action Fund later named its Twin Vision® library after Kenneth Jernigan, who did so much to make more Braille materials available to the blind.

My children and I enjoyed these books, but they were not for sale, so we could not accumulate our own collection. We borrowed them from the libraries and were glad to have them. Many times, when either my daughter or son liked a particular book very much, we renewed its due date several times. Even then we finally had to return it with regret. Many of these books had been transcribed by volunteers, and there may have been only a single copy of some titles.

Today the American Action Fund, through its Braille Books for Blind Children program, gives older blind children Braille books they can keep for their very own. It also has a large lending library of Twin Vision® books which can be borrowed for babies and toddlers. But it is still difficult to purchase print/Braille storybooks for very young children. After my first visit with my new granddaughter, I began to look for print/Braille books to buy—books of our own that we could keep.

After searching without much luck, I attended the Convention of the National Federation of the Blind of Ohio and found a sale of print/Braille books. A blind, fifth-grade child and her mother, who was

President of our Ohio blind parents group, had made an agreement. Macy had collected quite a number of books which she no longer read. They are for third graders and below.

Macy reads lots of Braille and started very young with these special books. Macy decided to sell her old books for $5 each—keeping half the income for herself and giving the other half to our Ohio parents organization. Mom was the saleswoman.

It was a wonderful collection of 60 or 70 books, including quite a number of classics like *Little Red Riding Hood*, Walt Disney's *101 Dalmatians*, and *Hansel and Gretel*. I was one of several people attending that convention who were thrilled with the opportunity to buy some of these books, and I did. The books were gone far before the end of the convention. It was a good convention, but the books were an important part of it for me.

After I returned home from a trip, my son called to see if I would baby-sit Friday evening. Nothing could have given me more pleasure. He warned me that Jordyn had given some sitters trouble by screaming. She has had colic. Well, I thought, she won't be the first person to scream at me. I just won't worry about it. But Jordyn was charm personified!

We played with a Clifford dog. We played with a Santa Claus Ferby. We talked to the baby in the mirror. And we read from one of the print/Braille books, *Curious George*. She took a nap, got a clean diaper, had a bottle, and we read some more.

Jordyn is now three months old and is just as interested in these bright pages as the baby I had held at her house three months ago. Only this time I had a small shelf of books to choose from, and I could read the text out loud from any of them. The bookshelf is under the mantle beside the fireplace right next to the rocking chair with the rocking footstool.

When her parents came to get her, Jordyn laughed out loud for almost the first time. Her mother had heard it that afternoon, but her father and I were delighted. She laughed several times—I think to tell me she had enjoyed the evening as much as I had.

I hope Jordyn will also enjoy having her own bookshelf at Grandma's house and reading her own special books when she comes to visit.

The National Federation of the Blind has led the way in changing many things about blindness during the last thirty years since my children were babies and the thirty years before that, too. Education for blind children is improving. Employment opportunities are much better. Newspapers will soon be available by telephone to every blind person in the country because of the work of the Federation. These are a few of many changes, and I appreciate them all. Sometimes, though, the little things matter as much as the big ones. I look forward to spending more special times with my granddaughter. Among other things, we will be reading print/Braille books from Jordyn's bookshelf.

PIGEONS, SEALS, AND NAVIGATING ON LAND

By Anthony R. Candela

The Kernel Books make their mark in many ways. Anthony Candela is a blind man who lives in California. He has not been an active member of the National Federation of the Blind, but he has read and been touched by the Kernel Books.

Mr. Candela wrote to ask me if he could submit a story, and I'm glad that he did. He writes with sparkle and sensitivity. He has clearly absorbed the Federation's philosophy of independence and self-respect and lives it on a daily basis. Here is what he has to say:

One day, while on my way to work in San Francisco, I had a most irksome thing happen to me. I suddenly found myself alone in the deserted recesses of a bus terminal that I used every day. I had no idea where I was or which way to go to get to the street. Taking an educated guess, I struck out in a direction I thought might lead to a more populated part of the station. Things got bleaker as I found that I had wandered into a rather quiet place.

All I had for company were the cement walls that seemed to typify the station's maze-like structure. A remnant from the past when trains were the dominant form of public transit, railroad tracks once ran into the several side-corridors that honeycomb the station. Although the tracks were removed long ago, the building retains dozens of smooth ramps and pedestrian walkways, leading to a variety of places within this venerable old edifice.

Echoing from several feet away and to my relief, I heard a voice call out, "Do you need help?" I called back, "Yes, I'm simply trying to get out of here."

When the man approached, I grew a little nervous. He smelled terrible—in my mind, a sure sign of someone who is homeless and, I imagined, a person who could rob me. I suspected I might need to raise my guard.

I thought to myself, "This shouldn't be happening. I travel this route every day. I guess I shouldn't have assumed I was let off the bus on the usual platform." I smiled as I realized that I didn't know the bus station as well as I thought. I marveled how the dozen or so people who had gotten off the bus with me had disappeared so quickly. Was it because they knew something I didn't?

In general, most people experience the physical environment as predictable and logical. We believe implicitly that the ground will remain solid, buildings will remain upright and permanent, and streets will not suddenly shift direction. We expect that, if we use common sense and safety precautions, we will arrive at our destinations unscathed.

Untoward world or geological events can temporarily shake our confidence, but, generally, most of us believe that, so long as we can see what is in front of us, we will remain safe. How, then, do those who cannot see figure out how to get along in environments that are not always predictable?

When I was a youngster, I had a small amount of vision. As the years went by, this vision slowly deteriorated and, although I remember many visual images, I can no longer see more than light and occasional shadow. Like many people, it took time for me to learn that blind people do indeed travel their neighborhoods, cities, towns, back roads, hiking trails, mountain paths, and, yes, even labyrinthine bus terminals.

I learned to supplement common sense with a collection of special skills to compensate for lack of vision. I can attest that anyone can learn these skills, but, because most people believe their eyesight is the only tool they need, they usually don't. I, too, resisted learning how to do things in nonvisual ways. If not for the encouragement of blind mentors who convinced me that I was slowing myself down by insisting upon using my less than adequate eyesight, I would not have learned how to use my other senses and my powers of perception and reasoning nearly as well or as quickly.

The man approached and jovially announced that he would show me how to get out of the bus station. He asked, "Where do you want to go?" I hesitated, thinking, "Do you really want to get involved with this fellow?"

Deciding that I could handle anything that might happen, I told him the names of the streets that formed the intersection nearest to my destination. He considered for a moment and then lightly said he didn't know where I meant, but not to worry. After getting to the street, he plotted, we would ask someone for directions. Then he surprised me, saying rather authoritatively, "Take my elbow, and we'll be on our way." I did, and we quite smoothly commenced our journey. Realizing that this man seemed to have a natural 'feel' for how to walk with a blind person, I began to relax.

Walking down three flights of stairs, turning left then right and then left again, we emerged, at last, into fresh air. Happily noticing that the sun was shining and feeling its delightful warmth on my right temple, I calculated that we had left the terminal on its extreme western wing, and we needed to travel straight ahead (north) until we met a busy street. At that point, I estimated, we would then need to turn right and walk east a few blocks to head in the direction I needed to go.

The man seemed genuine when he said, "I really appreciate your ability to tell direction from the sun." Before I could feel gratified by his compliment, he re-kindled my suspicions when he said, "When I was a Navy Seal, we learned all sorts of survival strategies, including some we could use if we became disabled."

Frankly, I found it hard to believe this disheveled, smelly, and somewhat scrawny man could have possibly been a Seal. Yet his mild and lighthearted demeanor belied his physical appearance. He asked, "How do you navigate and travel safely?" I said I would explain as we walked. I asked him when he served in the Navy. He said, "I was in Vietnam. I'm almost 60 years old."

We walked a block and stopped at a corner. Still unsure of my guide and hearing someone approaching, I hailed a pedestrian and asked for the name of the street in front of us. Learning which one it was, I was heartened when my benefactor confirmed my reckoning and suggested we turn right. I told him that even the best blind traveler occasionally relies on the assistance of others.

He replied that the Seals taught him that you must always look out for each other.

"Teamwork is the name of the game," he said. "By the way," he asked, "Where exactly do you want to go?" "The bagel shop," I answered somewhat sheepishly. "I always stop there on my way to the office."

We walked two blocks. Suddenly and seemingly out of nowhere, I was surprised by the familiar coos and characteristic wing flaps of a flock of pigeons scrambling to rise from the ground where they were feeding. I then remembered with delight that this was the spot directly in front of the main entrance to the bus terminal.

In my everyday travels to this station, I had managed to figure out that the pigeons (admittedly, an unorthodox environmental cue) seem always to dine in the same place. It took me a while to believe it was true, but eventually I allowed myself to use this natural phenomenon to help me determine my exact location.

Feeling a surge of triumph, now that I knew exactly where we were, I said to my new friend, "I can go the rest of the way on my own." "No" he insisted, "I'll take you to the bagel shop." I thought to myself, "I'll buy him breakfast."

Nearing the bagel shop, we stopped to wait at an intersection. My guide asked me how I could possibly cross these streets by myself. He was particularly concerned because the main street intersected two sets of perpendicular streets at an acute angle.

I explained that, with practice and a lot of listening to automobile traffic movement patterns, a blind person can learn to target the opposite corner and cross with parallel traffic. When in doubt, I explained, listening for the footsteps of other pedestrians and, if necessary, requesting assistance, would be appropriate ways to stay on course. He chuckled at my nautical reference.

Arriving at the bagel shop, its familiar aroma filling me with comfort this particular morning, I was surprised when my companion slapped me on the shoulder and said, "Here you are. Have a good day." He told me he thought the skills I used were quite interesting. "You're a 'top gun,'" he said. As he turned to leave, I saluted him, turned away, and entered the shop to purchase my morning repast.

LESSONS OF CAMP MERRY HEART

by Daniel B. Frye

Dan Frye is a former National Federation of the Blind scholarship winner. He is now an attorney practicing law in Washington State. One summer during his college years he served as a camp counselor. Here is how he describes the experience:

During the summer of 1988 I got a job as a Senior Counselor at Camp Merry Heart, an Easter Seal-sponsored challenge and recreational retreat for physically disabled people in the rural outskirts of Hackettstown, New Jersey. Hoping to enhance my résumé by successfully working a summer job, I left the comfortable familiarity of college life in South Carolina,

Daniel B. Frye

boarded a northbound Greyhound, and set out on a summer adventure which promised to be exciting and instructive.

In an effort to make a good first impression, I called the camp supervisor from the Greenville, South Carolina, bus station and politely declined her offer to have a camp representative pick me up at the Port Authority in New York City. I explained that I was confident of my ability to make the necessary transfer to the commuter bus which would take me directly to Hackettstown. She reluctantly resigned herself to the travel arrangements that I— her new twenty-year-old blind summer employee—proposed, and we agreed to meet the next morning for staff orientation.

While alone in the darkness of night on a sixteen-hour bus journey which would transport me from the tranquil South to the teeming North, I had ample opportunity to entertain a range of feelings from eagerness to apprehension.

While my spirits were bolstered by the possibilities of the summer to come, I simultaneously felt the anxiety inherent in being a newly independent young adult traveling to an unfamiliar region of the country where I would assume the responsibilities of a vaguely defined summer position.

I hoped that I could do the job well. I hoped that I would fit in and develop pleasant working relationships with my colleagues and the campers. And, most of all, I hoped that my blindness would not be used as a justification to bar me from completely fulfilling my obligations as a staff member or represent a barrier to my participation in camp life.

At some point in the wee hours of the morning I concluded that further analysis of my emotions would be fruitless, and I drifted off to sleep, only to be awakened by the announcement, "Arriving, New York City."

My transfer to the commuter bus was uneventful, and after settling in to the rustic, un-air-conditioned log cabin which would be my home for the next several months, I reported to the camp dining hall for staff orientation. I was encouraged by my initial reception from the other counselors (most of whom were also college students on summer vacation), but it became apparent immediately that the camp's management did not share their faith in my ability to function as a capable staff member.

Despite my certifications in CPR and Advanced Swimming by the American Red Cross, I was not permitted to participate in "Life Drills," a procedure which involved four staff members—tethered equidistantly to a rope stretched across the camp lake—diving, exploring, and resurfacing together in search of a hypothetical accident victim.

I protested that, in addition to being competent in swimming and first aid, I would face minimal safety risk because this operation was executed in teams of four, that we were all secured by a life rope, and that most of the underwater exploration was accomplished tactilely because of the lake's murkiness.

The management decision to forbid my service as a counselor in the integrated day camp, which catered to both disabled and non-disabled campers, resulted in a second restriction on my full conduct of camp responsibilities. The rationale offered for this policy was that vision was essential to the successful supervision of the more active camping population. These and other exclusions became the norm throughout my summer employment at Camp Merry Heart.

I privately resolved to stick it out until my employment was scheduled to end in mid-August. Frequently, however, my spirits wavered, and I was tempted to offer my premature resignation. Ultimately I decided that the image of blind people would be better served by my decision to stay with my employer, conducting the tasks assigned to me with efficiency and dignity while trying to educate and advocate for improvement of management's attitudes about blindness. I reasoned that, if I did my job well and used the art of diplomacy to enlighten camp leaders about my disability, I could acquit myself with distinction and preserve opportunities for any future blind candidate seeking employment with Camp Merry Heart.

As the days melted into weeks, I slowly settled into the established routine of camp life. Waking to reveille at 6:00 a.m., I helped my campers prepare for the day ahead. I escorted them to flag-raising, accompanied them to breakfast, and returned with them to our quarters for morning cabin cleaning.

By 8:30 a.m. we'd leave for camp exercises, field games, arts and crafts, swimming, and other traditional camping activities. Once during every week-long camp session, we'd conduct an overnight outdoor camping excursion complete with cooking over camp fires and sleeping under the stars.

Our evenings would usually conclude with an assembly of sorts, in which campers put on plays, participated in talent shows, or simply socialized with each other in the central dining hall. Lights went out at 10:00 p.m., and weary counselors on night call duty would quietly meet on the front porches of their cabins and talk about home, life at college, and personal dreams and generally spend time building friendships with one another.

It was those relaxing summer evenings, long after campers had retired, that I came to cherish most. In whispers so as not to disturb the campers, my friends and I would discuss the pros and cons of the Merry Heart experience. Sometimes we would analyze my dissatisfaction, frustration, and exasperation with the attitudes exhibited by

Merry Heart leaders about my blindness. We agreed that it was unfortunate and ironic that such a lack of confidence in an independent blind person prevailed at a camp which prided itself in its belief in and support of "true achievement" for disabled people.

Near the summer's end I told a few of my friends of my intention to use part of my salary to explore some of the quaint towns within a several-hundred-mile radius of Hackettstown. Preferring the allure of New York City's bright lights, everyone to whom I had extended an invitation to accompany me for this weekend declined my offer, so I made arrangements to travel alone.

Despite my educational efforts throughout the summer, a couple of my friends and a member of the camp's administration expressed some surprise and concern that I had not altered my plans once I learned that nobody else was joining me on my trip. They asked me how I thought I would manage without somebody around to orient me to my surroundings and whether it didn't make sense to identify a specific destination so that I could have some idea of what to expect. Realizing that changing ingrained notions about blindness is always a slow process, I patiently explained that with my cane and some cash I would be fine and that the absence of plans was largely what made the adventure attractive.

On a Friday afternoon after all the campers had bid their farewells and the facilities were shut down for another two-day respite, I got a ride in to Hackettstown, asked the ticket agent what the final destination of the New York City commuter bus was, and purchased a ticket to Wilkes-Barre, Pennsylvania.

Several hours later I was comfortably ensconced in a small hotel. Having ordered a pizza, I luxuriously stretched out across my king-size bed and contented myself watching former Texas Governor Ann Richards deliver a televised nomination speech for Democratic presidential candidate Michael Dukakis at the 1988 Democratic national convention. Throughout the rest of the weekend I watched movies, swam, explored the town and its history, and found other amusements with which to occupy myself. In short, I had a great time.

During these days of recreational solitude, I had considerable opportunity to reflect upon the events of the summer. I smiled inwardly at the knowledge that I was growing up and that the philosophy about blindness to which I had always subscribed really seemed to work. Having determined to visit Wilkes-Barre on a whim, I found that I was managing well and that blindness was not much of an issue. Further, I concluded that I was actually quite satisfied with my successful performance in what could be fairly characterized as my first real job.

Even when I pondered the turbulent and bittersweet aspects of the summer's experience, I realized with pride that I had been equal to the challenge, and I noted with corresponding sobriety that as I matured it would be necessary for me to develop sophistication in effectively addressing social misunderstandings about blindness. While vacationing in Wilkes-Barre, I reaffirmed that the best way to accomplish this would be to play an active part in the National Federation of the Blind.

As this contemplative weekend drew to an end and I prepared to return to Camp Merry Heart to finish the last several weeks of my summer job, I decided with great certainty that I was glad I had come.

FRAN ALLISON AND ME

by Stephen O. Benson

Stephen Benson serves as President of the NFB of Illinois and as a Member of the National Federation of the Blind's Board of Directors. The following recollection of a childhood event reminds us how far we have come and how far we still have to go on our journey to freedom. Here is what he says:

My mother's formal education extended through at least part of seventh grade. She became a very clever artist who created the most wonderful pieces out of virtually nothing: buttons, feathers, copper wire, colored tissue paper, and more. She brought animals to life on canvas with oils. She did still lifes and landscapes in several media. Her silver point and Japanese brush paintings were excellent. Her favorite

Stephen O. Benson

medium was water color. I am pleased to know that her paintings and other works grace homes from coast to coast and border to border.

When I was a year and a half old, she and I moved from a small western Illinois town to Chicago. Shortly after that move doctors determined that retinitis pigmentosa would severely limit my vision and would eventually result in blindness.

I have no doubt that my mother was sorry to learn that my eye condition would result in blindness; that is the usual reaction to such news. But she was not destroyed by the fact that her only child would never have normal vision. Instead she proceeded to plot a course that would expose her young son to a rich variety of life-preparing experiences.

My mother was concerned that I might be reluctant to socialize, so she steered me to involvement in Cub Scouts and Boy

Scouts, to Saturday Red Cross swimming classes, and to roles in school plays even when I was in first grade.

In the late forties she took puppetry classes at Hull House under the direction of a nationally known puppeteer, Hans Schmitt. She learned to make hand puppets and costumes and stages including sets, props, and lighting. She taught me to do the same, but I was more interested in the performance end of puppetry. I became a part-time professional puppeteer, performing for seventeen years.

My interest in puppetry began to blossom in the very late forties and early fifties when my mother took me to see *Kukla, Fran, and Ollie*, one of the classic children's programs on early television. I was captivated by these puppet characters and thoroughly charmed by Fran Allison. My mother and I were frequent members of the live audience, and Fran became very friendly toward us.

By 1953 I was thoroughly immersed in Braille at Alexander Graham Bell School, one of Chicago's model schools. Celebrities and political dignitaries frequently visited our classroom. On such visits the blind students were required to stand at the right-hand side of our desks and greet the principal, who ordinarily ushered guests around the school.

One day a small group entered our classroom, and the prescribed ritual ensued. All at once one of the visitors stepped away from the rest, walked up to me, put her arms around me, and greeted me warmly. It was Fran Allison. She was as happy to see me as I was to see her. We were equally surprised. She spent a few extra minutes talking with each student in the room. She was genuinely warm and gracious, and all of my classmates enjoyed our meeting with a real live television personality.

Our resource room teacher (I'll call her Mrs. Q), had a different reaction. After the visitors had moved on to another classroom, Mrs. Q approached my desk and said, "What right do you have to know somebody like Miss Allison?" To say that I was shocked understates the situation. But I understood what she meant. For, you see, Mrs. Q was rich. She and her husband owned a string of race horses, and she drove to school in a luxury car. I was a poor kid from a single-parent home, and I was blind. Mrs. Q's message was clear: poor blind kids should stay in their places.

Mrs. Q's behavior was unacceptable and could have been devastating to me, except that my classmates and I viewed her with healthy measures of disdain and ridicule, for this was not her only display of contempt for blind kids. I don't believe any of us told our parents of incidents such as this one; it just wasn't done in those days.

In a strange way Mrs. Q's behavior helped to prepare my classmates and me for what we would encounter as adults from many agencies for the blind and from some members of the public.

The National Federation of the Blind has had measurable, positive influence on public attitudes toward blindness and blind people through the Kernel Books and other publications. The general public is now much more accepting of the idea that blind people compete on an equal basis, but there is much work yet to be done. So blind people and right-thinking sighted people must simply roll up our collective sleeves and get on with the task of improving all our lives by providing better education and training for all blind people.

My Life

by Bob Munz

Not all of us are cut out to be lawyers, teachers, or engineers. But nearly all of us have the capacity to do useful work and contribute to the world in which we live.

Unfortunately, blind people who are not superstars are frequently pushed off to the sidelines, relegated needlessly to inactivity or substandard employment. Bob Munz tells just such a story. Far too many years passed before he really got the help he needed. Here is what he has to say about how the National Federation of the Blind helped to turn his life around:

I work for Price Costco. I have my own apartment. I've had a girlfriend for thirteen years who is true to me. But my life wasn't always so good. When I was little, I slept on the floor at home with my four brothers. I didn't know what a bed or a pillow was until I went away to school. The school bought me clothes because my mother couldn't afford to.

When I went home on weekends, my brothers would take my new clothes and send me back to school in rags. After that happened a couple of times the school had me go back to the dorm an hour before we left for the weekend and change back to the rags so I could leave my new clothing at school.

At the school for the blind I was not taught very much Braille because I could still see a little. I left the school in 1970, not having learned enough Braille to use in a job. Then I was sent to an adult training program in New Hyde Park, New York, where I asked if I could learn Braille. They said no.

Bob Munz

They thought I didn't need Braille, and they would decide for me what I did and did not need. I didn't agree with them, but I didn't know what to do.

After I left New Hyde Park (which was a one-year program), I decided to leave my mother's house. A social worker talked to my mother about my entering a boarding situation where the landlady was also blind.

I don't know why her blindness was relevant to my blindness. It may have been that since both of us were blind the social worker thought we'd have things in common. We had nothing in common. It was while I lived at this boarding house that I worked for seven years in a sheltered workshop, in which I often made only forty cents an hour.

In 1986, I left the sheltered workshop and found a job on my own in a supermarket. I lived in the boarding house from 1972 to 1989, when I had a serious accident which pretty much took away the rest of my usable vision.

It took me a year to recover from that accident, and the result was that I couldn't go back to my previous job collecting carts in a supermarket. I was unemployed for three years until I got the chance to go to the National Federation of the Blind training center in Louisiana.

There, more than 25 years after leaving high school, I finally got the kind of help I really needed. I learned cooking, typing, mobility, Braille, and even fun things like swimming and fishing. After I came back from Louisiana, I got my current job. In this job, I work on the floor folding clothes, and in the back behind the counter preparing and serving hot dogs and other foods. I also go outside to make sure everything is clean and in place.

My girlfriend's father is trying to persuade me to go into a group home because he does not think that blind people can function on their own. I have my own apartment, a job, and a girlfriend. I do my own shopping and cleaning.

The only thing I do get help with is reading my mail and writing letters. So my answer to my girlfriend's father is, I have no reason to live in a group home or work in sheltered employment when I am making it in the real world.

If not for the National Federation of the Blind I would not believe in myself, and I would not be where I am today. I know I would never have left my forty-cents-an-hour sheltered workshop job and had the confidence to do the work and live the life I now enjoy so much. It's truly a different world for me.

THE BETTER GIFT

By Peggy Elliott

Peggy Elliott is Second Vice President of the National Federation of the Blind. She is a graduate of Yale Law School and practices law in Grinnell, Iowa. Her stories have appeared in many previous Kernel Books. In this volume she tells how she overcame the thing that frightened her most when, as a teen-ager, she became totally blind. Here is what she has to say:

When I lost my sight as a teen-ager, one of the scariest things for me was the thought that I had lost my physical freedom: the ability to move where I wanted, when I wanted, and to do it safely. Since I could no longer see, I was sure that I was limited to a few very familiar places. I hated the thought. This meant I couldn't work, couldn't shop, couldn't meet friends for dinner—couldn't do all the things others do. Or, so I thought.

Fortunately, I was wrong. When I met the National Federation of the Blind, I found that I could learn to move about safely and go where I wanted when I wanted. I've been doing it for thirty years now, and I have found that my physical freedom is only limited by my own choices. Blindness doesn't limit me. Sure, learning to use the cane takes practice. But the hardest thing to learn is to trust yourself, your head, and your cane to find the path and do it safely.

When I was in my twenties, I was still learning to trust myself. One experience I remember helped to teach me to rely on myself and to go for it.

I was in Washington, D.C., in conjunction with the National Convention of the National Federation of the Blind. At

Peggy Elliott

about noon, a group of us decided to visit our Iowa Congressional offices—just drop in and say "Hi."

The buses scheduled to take us back to the convention site were to park at the very western edge of the Capitol grounds and depart at 4:00 p.m. sharp. No exceptions. We had almost four hours. No sweat. We could do it. Although, speaking of sweat, the day was a scorcher, reaching temperatures over 100 degrees, which were exaggerated by Washington's humidity and the vast swaths of concrete paving and hard-surface buildings all around us. Still, no sweat. We were in our nation's capital and were going to take full advantage of the experience.

I had worked one summer in Washington and sort of knew my way around the long and twisting halls of the office buildings. The three other people in my group were two sighted friends and their toddler daughter, riding in a stroller. We moved from office to office with my suggesting routes that kept us inside, using the tunnel system, and which would also avoid use of stairs to make the stroller's progress easier. We had a good time and enjoyed finding the Iowa flags outside our Congressmen's doors. We weren't watching the time that carefully.

At twenty minutes to four, we emerged from the last office and took stock. We had visited every office and managed to follow a logical progression through the buildings, never backtracking, and ending up at the extreme southeastern corner of the Capitol grounds. We had a fifteen-minute walk ahead of us, twenty minutes to departure time, oppressive heat outside, and a child in a stroller.

I told my friends that I knew a way to get from where we were to the west side of the Capitol building without a single step or curb. The path was entirely underground, and they would have to trust that I knew my way since there would be no landmarks until we emerged from the Capitol about five minutes before bus time. The alternative, I explained, was for us to go overland, go down at least one long flight of outside stairs, and use sidewalks with the necessity of crossing numerous streets to reach the bus. My inside route was smooth, used tunnels which were at angles, and would be faster if they wanted me to guide. The outside route would be along straight lines with square corners, taking longer, but they could see where they were.

My two friends impatiently cut me off. They pointed out that they had been following me all afternoon to everyone's satisfaction and would I please hush up and start leading them on the inside, smooth, air-conditioned route.

We took off, flying down the tunnels of two large buildings, zooming onto and off of elevators, and emerging with about seven minutes to spare at the western side of the Capitol.

I stopped and turned to my two friends, explaining that we were now facing west at the farthest point we could travel inside and that they should help now to pick the quickest way to the buses since they would be able to identify the sidewalks that led most speedily to our transportation.

Both my friends stood there, silent. I asked why. One replied: "We can't see any buses." Oh, great, I thought. The buses took off early. Then I began to worry that my wonderful guiding skills weren't so great after all and that I had brought us to the wrong side of the huge Capitol building. Neither of my sighted friends said anything, but I was beginning to formulate apologies for my failure. We all just stood there, defeated.

Only *I* thought we were standing there defeated. Apparently, my two friends were continuing to scan the area to the west that I had indicated they should study. Suddenly, one of my friends started gesturing wildly, pointing and laughing. She shouted, "Look! There are some blind people! Follow those blind people! They know where they're going!" We stepped lively, "followed the blind people," and found the buses hidden by foliage. We were the last four people on, but we made it.

As we rode back to the convention, I thought about what had just happened. My friends had a child to protect from excessive heat, jostling, and discomfort. They had trusted me to guide them along a path which would provide maximum protection for their child rather than choosing the route for which they would have been navigators but in the baking sun and with uncomfortable jostling for their daughter.

When my knowledge no longer served us, they found other blind people to follow, trusting that their blind friends knew what was up. These were capable professional people and parents, and their attitude was uniformly that they believed in the abilities of their blind friends. Sometimes even more than I believed in myself.

I think that may have been the day I finally quit worrying about whether I could get around safely—and do it when I wanted and where I wanted. I got the family to the bus in comfort. They gave me that last little bit of confidence to quit worrying about getting around. I think I got the better gift.

You can help us spread the word...

...about our Braille Readers Are Leaders contest for blind schoolchildren, a project which encourages blind children to achieve literacy through Braille.

...about our scholarships for deserving blind college students.

...about Job Opportunities for the Blind, a program that matches capable blind people with employers who need their skills.

...about where to turn for accurate information about blindness and the abilities of the blind.

Most importantly, you can help us by sharing what you've learned about blindness in these pages with your family and friends. If you know anyone who needs assistance with the problems of blindness, please write:

Marc Maurer, President
National Federation of the Blind
1800 Johnson Street, Suite 300
Baltimore, Maryland 21230-4998

Other Ways You Can Help the National Federation of the Blind

Write to us for tax-saving information on bequests and planned giving programs.

OR

Include the following language in your will:

"I give, devise, and bequeath unto National Federation of the Blind, 1800 Johnson Street, Suite 300, Baltimore, Maryland 21230, a District of Columbia nonprofit corporation, the sum of $_____ (or "___ percent of my net estate" or "The following stocks and bonds:_____") to be used for its worthy purposes on behalf of blind persons."

Your Contributions Are Tax-deductible